Scottish Castles

First published in 1998 by Wayland Publishers Ltd,
61 Western Road, Hove, East Sussex BN3 1JD, England

Find Wayland on the Internet at
http://www.wayland.co.uk

British Library Cataloguing in Publication Data
Dargie, Richard
    Scottish Castles Through History
    1. Castles – Scotland – Juvenile literature
    2. Scotland – History – Juvenile literature
    I. Title II. Hook, Richard
    728.8'1'09411

ISBN 0 7502 2148 8

Editor: Carron Brown
Consultant: Donald Gunn, an Education Officer for
BBC Education Scotland
Designer: Joyce Chester
Production controller: Carol Titchener

Typeset in England by Joyce Chester
Printed and bound in Italy by G. Canale C.S.p.A, Turin

Picture Acknowledgements

Historic Scotland cover (top left), 19, 20; Robert
Harding/Tom Mackie *cover* (main picture), 21 (top);
Historic Scotland/Crown Copyright Reserved *cover*
(top), 19, 20, 36; Michael Holford 13, 15; National
Library of Scotland 17 (top); Scotland in Focus/JB 27;
/George Dey 31, /D. Farquhar 39, /E. Gabriel
17 (bottom), /R. Weir 30; Scottish Highland Photo
Library *contents page*, 8, /H.I.E *endpapers*, /Hugh Webster
39, /R. Weir 30; Still Moving Picture Company
/Doug Corrance 35, /Gerry Coutts 14, /Derek Laird
28, /STB 33, 41, /Paul Tomkins/STB 29; David
Williams 40; Woodmansterne 34, 38 /National Trust for
Scotland 21 (bottom), 24, 37, /Historic Buildings and
Monuments 9; 32.

Artwork supplied by: Kate Davenport castle cover and
chapter logo, 12; Richard Hook 6–7, 10–11, 12–13, 16,
18–19, 22–3, 25; Sallie Alane Reason 45.

Cover: [main] Caerlaverock Castle; [inset] A
reconstruction of a siege weapon used in the Middle
Ages.
Endpapers: Eilean Donan Castle on Loch Duich.
Contents page: The Iron Age broch at Mousa in the
Shetland Islands.

through History

Contents

Capturing the Castle, 1314

It was dark and there was little light from the clouded moon. Thirty men hid in the shadows at the foot of a towering cliff. Their leader gave a nod and the men spread out. It was time to look for the first handholds and begin the near-impossible climb up the sheer rock face.

The climbers made their way upwards in silence. They were Scots and their leader was the brave knight Sir Thomas Randolph, Earl of Moray. The castle on the crag had been in English hands since 1296. A large garrison of 350 soldiers had been ordered to hold Edinburgh for England's King Edward I.

For eighteen years, the Scots had been fighting to win back their freedom. Now they were led by a great warrior king, Robert the Bruce. Battles had been fought and castles had been besieged. The English had been thrown out of most of the land. Now Edinburgh was one of only four strongholds still in English hands.

The Earl of Moray's men climbed the steep walls of Edinburgh Castle and took the English troops by surprise.

The Earl of Moray knew he could never take the castle by force. The only chance was to take the English troops by surprise. Everyone believed the north cliff was too steep to be climbed. There were few sentries on that side of the castle. So that was Moray's route to the ramparts and over the walls. His men were skilled climbers and silent killers. The English troops were slaughtered in their beds.

The next morning the saltire of Scotland flew over Edinburgh Castle. The Scots smashed the walls and the gates so that the fortress could never be used by the English again. Then Moray rode north to meet his uncle, King Robert. Their next target was Stirling. There they would destroy the English army at the Battle of Bannockburn. It was spring 1314. The long War of Independence was coming to a close.

The First Forts

The early Celtic peoples of Scotland lived in a country that was wild and dangerous. Much of the country was covered by moor and thick forest. There were wild creatures such as wolves, bears and eagles. There was the danger of attack from rival tribes and from sea invaders. These early peoples needed to feel safe so they built strong forts to defend themselves.

The broch at Mousa was built by local farmers in the Shetland Islands over 2,500 years ago.

Some tribes built brochs. These were high, round towers made of stone. Some were more than 10 m high. The walls were 4 m thick and had no windows. The doorway was a low passage which was easy to defend. In times of trouble, the early farmers of Scotland could shelter here with their animals and their families. Many brochs survive today in the Northern and Western Isles.

This is an aerial view of an Iron Age hill-fort in the Cheviots.

Other tribes lived in crannogs. A crannog was a timber hut built on a loch, with the living area situated just above the surface of the water. The builders drove long timbers into the muddy bed of the loch to make a strong foundation. These were bound together to form a base. The crannog was linked to the mainland by a wooden path that could be cut in times of trouble. The crannogs at Loch Kinord in Aberdeenshire and at Loch Awe in Argyll can be seen easily today, and a reconstruction of a crannog has been built on Loch Tay in Perthshire.

Most Celtic tribes built their villages on top of a hill for safety. There are over 1,500 hill-forts in Scotland. Some had walls of heaped earth and turf with a wooden battlement on top. Others were vitrified – the walls were made of rubble encased in a timber framework. When the timber was set alight, the rubble melted and fused. This made the walls stronger. Some hill-forts, such as Traprain Law in East Lothian, were large enough to hold a small town of over 1,000 people. Most hill-forts were only used in times of trouble.

King Malcolm's Tower

Brochs, crannogs and hill-forts were the safe places of the early peoples of Scotland. In the years after AD 500, new kinds of fortresses were built. We know that the Pictish kings of northern Scotland built a strong fort made of high stone walls at the coastal shrine of Burghead. Burghead was a massive citadel which was also protected by outer walls, high wooden gates and deep ditches.

When Viking raiders began to attack Scotland's coasts after AD 795, some Picts built high, round towers as a place of refuge. The door to these towers was almost 5 m off the ground. In peacetime, the door was reached by a wooden stairway. This was burnt or destroyed in times of trouble. There are Pictish towers of this kind at Brechin in Angus and Abernethy in Perthshire.

Malcolm III was known by the Gaelic title of Canmore or 'great chieftain'. He became king in AD 1058. He was an able man who could speak Gaelic, English and French. Malcolm Canmore decided that his kingdom needed a permanent capital. He chose Dunfermline, which controlled the Firth of Forth. This was Scotland's most important sea-way in the Middle Ages.

At Dunfermline, Malcolm built a different kind of defence. Instead of a wooden palisade, it was a stone tower with battlements. It was probably the first stone castle in Scotland.

Malcolm's stone tower was the strongest in the Kingdom of the Scots.

Malcolm's wife, Queen Margaret, had lived in Europe and in England. Possibly she described the new kind of stone castles that were being built on the continent to her husband. The ruins of King Malcolm's stone tower can still be seen in the grounds of Dunfermline Abbey.

Malcolm also spent time strengthening the hill-fort at Din Eidyn in the Lothians. This became known as Edinburgh Castle. Queen Margaret died there in AD 1093. Her son, King David I, built a chapel in her memory in AD 1130. It still stands in the castle today.

The Norman Castle Builders

In the 1060s, new invaders came to the British Isles. These were the Normans from Normandy in France. By 1068, they had conquered England and were beginning to threaten the Scots. The Normans were well-trained soldiers. They were skilled cavalrymen and were protected by thick chain-mail armour. Malcolm Canmore and the kings of Scotland who followed him knew that they could not easily defeat the Normans. Instead, they made peace with them and began to use some Norman ideas.

The Normans built motte-and-bailey castles in order to control their estates.

After 1100, Norman lords were invited into Scotland to help run the kingdom. These lords were given grants of land or estates by the King of Scots. To control these lands they built a new kind of castle. This was the motte and bailey. A mound of earth was quickly built up. This was called a motte or hill. A wooden stockade was built around the motte. Inside the stockade, the Normans built a high, wooden tower as a look-out point. A second, outer wall was built. The courtyard inside this wall was called the bailey. Here there were stables, storehouses, barracks and sometimes a chapel. A ditch was often built around the bailey wall. This was filled with water as an extra defence.

Local villagers were often forced to build the mottes for the Norman knights. In time, the wooden defences were replaced by stone walls and a high, stone tower called a keep.

These Norman knights became defenders of the Scottish kingdom. Their names – Sinclair, Barclay, Ramsay, Fraser, Lindsay and Wallace – are common names in Scotland today. Two of these Norman families, the Bruces and the Stewarts, became Kings of Scotland. Many of the motte-and-bailey castles that they built can still be seen today. The wooden towers and buildings have long since disappeared but the earthworks remain. There are well-preserved mottes at Duffus in Moray, Urr in Dumfriesshire and at Inverurie in Aberdeenshire.

The First Stone Castles

Motte-and-bailey castles were made of wood, which meant that an attacking enemy could set them alight. After 1100, the Normans began to replace the wooden stockades with safer and stronger stone walls and battlements. At Balvenie Castle in Morayshire, the bailey was enclosed by a massive curtain wall over 2 m thick and 10 m high. At Duffus near Elgin, the builders tried to put a stone keep on top of the old earthen motte. The mound could not bear the load and the tower collapsed in a landslide.

Rothesay Castle was an important strongpoint in the wars between Scotland and Norway. It was captured by the Norse in 1230. It became Scottish again after 1263 when the Norwegian army was defeated at the Battle of Largs.

Many of the earliest stone castles were built on the west coast of Scotland. There were hardly any trees in that part of the country. Timber was scarce but plenty of stone was available.

The west coast was also the border between two kingdoms – Scotland and Norway. Since Viking times, Norwegians had lived on Scotland's west coast. It took hundreds of years of warfare before the Norwegians were forced out in AD 1263. Stone castles like Castle Sween in Kintyre were needed here for controlling this border.

Scotland had another dangerous enemy to the south. Many stone castles were built to defend the roads from England into Scotland. Some of these were very simple structures, such as Hermitage Castle in Liddesdale.

This grim fortress was built close to the English border in 1243. It was so menacing that the English King Henry III raised an army and went to war just to try and destroy it. In the Middle Ages, southern Scotland bristled with towers and castles. Some of these, such as Dirleton and Tantallon in East Lothian, were vast, expensive fortifications. Often they were based on the latest ideas about castle building from abroad.

The great stone bulk of Hermitage Castle controlled an important road from Scotland to the south.

The King's Safe Places

The key fortresses in Scotland were under the control of the king. These were the royal castles of Stirling, Edinburgh, Roxburgh and Dumbarton. Stirling Castle controlled the roads north into the rich lands of Fife and Angus. Edinburgh and Roxburgh were important border defences. The castle on the volcanic rock at Dumbarton dominated the Firth of Clyde.

Castles were often run for the king by a group of trusted officials called sheriffs. It was their job to keep the castles ready for war. They had to raise money by taxing the farmers who worked on the king's land. These taxes were used to buy weapons and pay the wages of the castle guard. In time of war, it was the sheriff's job to hold a wapinschaw. This was an inspection of all the men in the area who were fit enough to fight in the king's army. The sheriff also acted as a judge in the Great Hall of the castle, hearing cases and punishing the guilty.

Sheriffs had to be loyal to the king and have a good knowledge of the land.

Some castles were built by kings for their own private use. At Lumphanan in Aberdeenshire, you can see the remains of a small fortress called the Peel. Legends link it to the old Celtic king of Scotland called Macbeth. Much later it was used by the medieval kings of the Bruce and Stewart families. It was a safe place for the king and his friends to stay when they were hunting deer in the Cairngorm forests.

King Robert the Bruce and his wife, Queen Isabella of Mar, in a picture drawn in 1600.

Kildrummy Castle

One of the strongest castles in Scotland was Kildrummy in Strathdon. In 1306, Robert the Bruce sent his wife and daughter to Kildrummy for safety. It was besieged by an English army but the castle was well defended and well supplied. However, the castle blacksmith was a traitor who set fire to the grain store. The flames weakened the castle walls and the English took it. The royal family were captured and taken to England as prisoners. They were held hostage there for the next ten years.

Siege Attack!

Many castles were so strong that they could not be captured by direct attack. Instead, the attackers laid siege. The besiegers made sure that no food or weapons got into the castle. The castle drawbridge was burnt by firing flaming arrows at it. Trenches were dug around the castle so that the defenders could not break out into the open countryside and collect food. Tunnels were dug under the castle walls. When the wooden tunnel supports were burnt, the tunnel collapsed, bringing down a section of the wall. The attackers surged through this gap in the castle's defences.

As many of Scotland's main castles were built on rock, besiegers had to try different ways of attack. In 1304, King Edward I of England tried to capture Stirling Castle. Thirteen siege engines were brought to the walls of Stirling. One weapon threw huge lead balls at the castle. The lead was stripped from the roof of St Andrew's Cathedral in Fife and melted down to make these balls. Another weapon hurled huge balls of blazing cotton cloth and tar on to the roofs of the houses inside the castle. This was called Greek Fire and it was a much-feared weapon.

This replica of a medieval siege engine can be seen at Caerlaverock Castle near Dumfries.

Edward finally ordered his men to build a new siege engine called the War Wolf. It threw iron balls which were over 140 kg in weight. These made great holes in the inner walls of the castle and forced the small Scots garrison to surrender to the English.

Stirling Castle was attacked by the latest weapons of war in the Great Siege of 1304.

Siege Engines

Three main kinds of siege engine were used in the Middle Ages. One was the mangonel which was like a giant catapult. It could propel a huge iron ball into the wooden gates of a castle. The trebuchet was a giant sling that hurled stones or metal balls at the walls. Siege towers were wooden frames which were covered in wet leather to stop them catching fire. Troops climbed up their frames on to the castle battlements.

Defending the Battlements

When a castle was attacked, the defenders could hurl stones, hot water and boiling oil at the attackers below. They could set fire to the enemy's wooden siege towers and could push away the enemy's scaling ladders. The Scots in Rothesay Castle did these things in 1230 when they were attacked by a Norse army. However, the castle was taken and the defenders were slaughtered. The answer was to prepare ahead of a siege.

A well-designed castle could be held by a small garrison. Sixty Scottish troops defended Caerlaverock Castle for weeks against the whole English army in AD 1300. Walls had to be thick enough to withstand battering from catapult stones. The walls at Bothwell Castle were over 30 m high and almost 6 m thick in places.

Castle gates were a weak point where the enemy could use their battering rams. Some castles defended their gatehouse by drawing up the bridge that led to it. Some castles had a portcullis – a metal grille that was raised by iron chains. The Scots developed their own style of gate called a yett. This was a criss-cross of iron strips which held the front wooden gates firm. If the attackers broke through, archers could fire at them through the gaps in the yett.

Many Scottish castles had special wooden galleries that stuck out beyond the castle wall. They allowed the defenders to drop stones down on the attackers below. These galleries were called machicolations. Craigmillar Castle (left) was so important for the defence of Edinburgh that the machicolations were built into the castle walls in stone.

The towers at Caerlaverock Castle still show part of their machicolations.

Some castles had a murder hole. This was a stone corridor between the inner and outer gate. An attacking enemy was allowed into the murder hole and then the gates were shut. The archers above could kill the men below one at a time.

Defenders always tried to make the siege last as long as possible. There was always the chance that the attackers would run out of supplies or that plague would break out in their camp. If the siege lasted all summer, the attackers would eventually go home. Medieval armies did not like fighting over the cold winter months.

A yett, the Scottish style of gate, at Crathes Castle.

The Castle Laird

The great nobles of Scotland were given their land because they promised to be loyal to the king and to help him in wartime. Lords like the Earl of Argyll and the Earl of Huntly had vast estates and great power. They acted for the king, delivering justice and giving protection to the ordinary people. Often, there many castles on an important noble's land. These were run by smaller lords or lairds who were kinsmen of the noble.

The laird usually lived in the castle keep with his family. He ate his meals in the Great Hall, sitting at the high table with his wife and friends.
A laird might look after the son of a neighbouring laird. The boy would be shown how to be a knight and how to run a castle household.

It was the duty of the laird to make sure that all men on his estate were trained and ready for war. Every man had to do forty days of service in the king's army. Lairds were often away from their own castle estate. They had to attend the King's Court or sit in the Scottish Parliament. When the laird was away, the castle was run by his chamberlain or deputy.

The laird was often a rich man and was expected to entertain his friends in style.

The farmers on the laird's estate paid rent each year to the laird. They did not often pay their rent with money. Instead, they gave him grain, salted meat and barrels of ale or whisky. These supplies were stored safely in the cool cellars of the castle. They could be used in times of famine or in a siege.

The laird was the local judge. Most local disputes were settled by his decision. Only the most serious cases, such as murder, went to be tried at the royal courts. Often, before a case started, the laird would secretly listen to defendants without them knowing he was there. He could watch and hear them, using 'the Laird's Lug' – a small hidden hole in the wall. This helped the laird to find out who was really telling the truth.

Castle Folk

Castles were always being improved, so the laird needed skilled craftsmen. High up on timber scaffolding, stone masons and carpenters would be working to make the castle more difficult to attack.

The blacksmith was one of the most important craftsmen in the castle. His job was to keep the horses on the laird's estate properly shod. He also worked with the castle armourer, making and repairing weapons and armour. Some castles employed a wheelwright who knew how to make wagons with iron-tyred wheels.

The laird's rooms were richly decorated and the ceilings were brightly coloured.

Castle walls were highly decorated with tapestry wall hangings and painted patterns drawn on the walls. The laird would employ a master painter to decorate the Great Hall and the main rooms used by his family. Often, a popular master painter would stay and work at a castle for a year or so before he moved on to his next job.

The castle kitchens were on the ground floor of the main keep tower. Sometimes, the kitchens and the bakehouse ovens were in a separate building, to prevent fire from spreading through the castle. The cook had different kinds of servants who worked beside him – spit-boys, washerwomen, serving lads and maids.

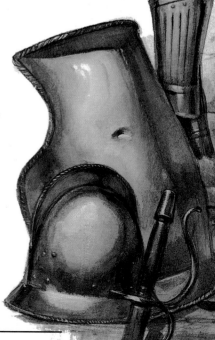

The lady of the castle had one or two maids who attended her in her rooms. Lairds might have a few musicians to entertain the family at dinner. Most castles had a priest who held services in the castle chapel. Some lairds had a jester. This was usually a close companion whose job was to entertain the laird. The last jester in Scotland was Jamie Fleming, who was known as the Laird of Udny's Fool.

Most castles had very few troops in them in times of peace. A laird might only have five or six trained men-at-arms in his service. They were skilled soldiers so they were expensive to hire. They acted as the laird's police on his estates and guarded the castle gatehouse. In wartime, the laird called on all the men on his estates to come to the castle and take up arms.

The blacksmith and the armourer were skilled and highly paid castle craftsmen.

The Rock

Edinburgh became a royal castle under Malcolm Canmore. By 1150, a burgh had grown up on the hillside leading down from the castle rock. In the Wars of Independence, the castle was captured several times. It was won back by the Scots for ever in 1341. Sir William Douglas and his men disguised themselves as merchants. They stopped their wagons under the castle gates so the English could not close them. Scottish troops rushed in and recovered the castle.

Under King James III, Edinburgh became the main royal stronghold in the kingdom. The king's papers, his crown and his sword of state were kept in Edinburgh for safety. Important prisoners were also held there. In 1479, the king's brother, the Duke of Albany, was accused of plotting treason and was shut up in the castle. He escaped from the castle by lowering himself down the rock using a rope tied to the bars of his prison window.

Stone of Destiny

Legend says that the Stone of Destiny is the pillow that Jacob used when he dreamt of Heaven in the Bible. Others say that the Stone was used by the ancient Scots when they appointed their new king. The King of Scots stood on the Stone and was lifted up by the Earls of Scotland so that his people could see him. The Stone was sacred to the medieval Scots. It was stolen by the English King Edward I in 1296. The Stone sat for many years beneath the English throne in Westminster Abbey. It returned to its rightful home in 1996 – exactly 700 years after it was stolen.

The Honours of Scotland, the royal crown and sword of state, have been held at Edinburgh for almost five hundred years. When the English invaded in 1650, they were briefly hidden at Dunnottar Castle and Kinneff Church near Aberdeen. When Scotland and England joined together in 1707, the Honours were locked in the Crown Room in Edinburgh Castle and the doors were walled up. They were forgotten about for over a hundred years. However, the Scottish writer Sir Walter Scott opened up the room in 1818 and the Honours were rediscovered.

The Honours have been on public display ever since, except for a brief period during the Second World War when they were secretly buried under the castle walls in case Scotland was invaded by the Germans.

Many Scots were killed in the First World War between 1914 and 1918. To honour their memory, the Scottish National War Memorial was built in the castle and opened in 1927.

When Edinburgh became Scotland's capital, the castle on the rock became an important royal palace.

Beneath the Castle Walls

Castles were a place of safety for merchants and their goods in times of trouble. At first, merchants paid the local laird for his protection. He charged them a fee to hold a market outside his castle walls. In time, the burghs grew in size and became richer. Merchants had to pay the king for the right to trade in a burgh.

The rich town of New Aberdeen grew up next to the castle. The oldest part of New Aberdeen was the Castlehill and the oldest street name of Castlegait dates back to 1107. There was a castle in Glasgow between the Cathedral and the farm lands of Cowcaddens. Every year from 1200 onwards, a fair lasting eight days was held around the castle. Booths sprang up and the town was packed with pedlars selling their wares. Country folk and some of the king's courtiers came to see the fair and to watch the travelling entertainers. Great crowds would gather to see acrobats and dancing bears at the burgh's Mercat Cross.

The heraldic emblem of Scotland, the unicorn, on the Edinburgh Mercat Cross.

In the countryside, many lairds created attractive gardens around their castles. Sometimes, this was done for practical reasons. Many castles had a walled kitchen garden. Here, sheltered from the wind, the laird's servants grew fruit and vegetables. Herbs were also grown. Some, like parsley and thyme, were used as seasonings in cooking. Others, like lavender, were used to freshen up the air in the stuffy castle living rooms.

Some country castles had decorative gardens. The most famous of these is at Edzell Castle in the Mearns which belonged to the Lindsay family. It was a very formal garden with rose beds and shaped hedges. As Lord Lindsay walked around his garden, he saw sets of sculptures and plaques on the walls. One set showed the Sun and the planets such as Mars and Venus. Another showed ancient goddesses who stood for the Arts and Sciences such as Music and Arithmetic. The third set showed Christian virtues such as Faith and Justice.

The gardens at Edzell Castle in the Mearns were designed with special scientific and ancient messages.

Highland Strongholds

The 'Wolf of Badenoch'

In the Middle Ages, the Highlands were troubled by outlaws. One of these was the fierce Alexander Stewart, known as the 'Wolf of Badenoch'. He led his army down the Moray coast, plundering the towns and burning Elgin Cathedral to the ground. His base was Lochindorb Castle, a square fortress on an island in the middle of a loch and a tough castle to attack.

In the Highlands, castles were built by the clan chiefs. Castles were needed to protect clan members and their property from enemies.

Highland castles often controlled an important pass into the glens. Castles such as Corgarff and Glenbuchat discouraged enemies from travelling through Strathdon. Carnassarie protected the rich farmlands of Kilmartin in Argyll. Kisimul sits in the middle of a harbour. This castle was built by the MacNeils so they could protect the Isle of Barra.

The MacDougall clan built eight castles along the Sound of Mull, an important sea passage. From Castle Duart they could watch the ships entering the Sound and signal if an enemy came.

Highland chiefs had the right of 'pit and gallows'. This meant they could imprison and execute criminals. Outlaws like Alexander Stewart made the Highlands a dangerous place. However, there was a greater threat than outlaws to the king's peace. This was the power of the MacDonald clan, the Lords of the Isles.

Kisimul Castle, first built around 1030.

Urquhart Castle by the shores of Loch Ness.

By 1400, they had built up an army of tough soldiers from the Highlands and Ireland. They built a fleet of ships called birlinns to control their island empire. In 1411, this Highland army marched on Aberdeen and was only stopped at the bloody Battle of Harlaw.

The kings of Scotland tried to make the Highlands more peaceful. To do this they built a massive fortress on the shores of Loch Ness. This was Urquhart Castle. From here, the king's troops tried to control the clan lands to the west.

The Blast of Guns

In the years after 1400, a new sound was heard at sieges throughout Europe. This was the blast of cannon. Cannon were able to knock down the high stone castle walls. Castle builders had to learn to make a new kind of defence, the artillery fort.

The first siege guns were made by welding long strips of iron together to make a barrel. This was reinforced by iron hoops. The cannon was then weighted by a block of heavy metal and fixed to a strong wooden frame. At first, cannon were used to fire blocks of shaped stone. Later, cannonballs were made of solid iron. The earliest cannon often did as much damage to their owners as they did to the enemy. In 1460, King James II was killed by one of his own guns when it exploded outside Roxburgh Castle.

Early siege guns were very heavy and difficult to move. Mons Meg was made in 1449, and was a gift to King James II.

Fort George

The biggest artillery fort in Europe can be seen at Fort George near Inverness. It was built in the eighteenth century. A Highland army marched south and almost captured London in 1745. The London government was so scared that it built forts across northern Scotland to keep the clans peaceful. Fort George was the largest of these. In modern money, Fort George cost over one billion pounds to build. It could hold 2,000 men and covered over 17 hectares. The artillery rampart alone was over a kilometre long. However, by the time it was completed in 1769, the Highlands were at peace.

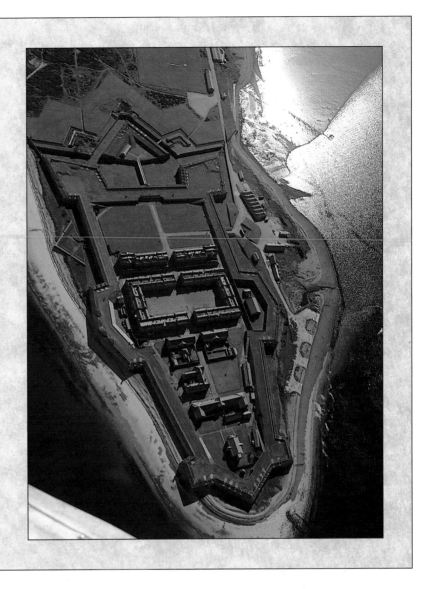

The most skilled cannon builders lived in France, Flanders and Holland. In 1511, King James IV sent his agents to France to hire gunne melters. A small group of skilled men travelled to Scotland to construct the king's artillery. Other guns were shipped over from Europe. One of these was Mons Meg, the giant cannon that now stands in Edinburgh Castle, which was made in Flanders.

Castle builders had to build lower, thicker walls that could withstand the impact of cannonballs. The new artillery forts had vast walls which were often packed with earth and rubble because cannonballs did less damage to this type of wall. Sieges became even longer and therefore they were more expensive, because the troops in the besieging army had to be paid and fed.

Castle into Palace

As warfare changed, the great stone castles were no longer needed for defence. The king and the Scottish nobles wanted to live in more comfortable buildings. Some of the old castles were turned into more pleasant residences.

King James IV turned Stirling Castle into a splendid palace for his Court. The Great Hall was richly decorated. Here the king received ambassadors from other countries. It was a room where the king could impress his guests. The castle had a Chapel Royal where the princes of Scotland were baptised. The Royal Library had over 600 books in six languages. King James V extended the royal apartments and had them decorated with statues. One was of the king himself and another showed the Devil.

King James IV (1473–1515) wanted splendid palaces which would reflect the growing wealth of his kingdom.

A Historic Flight

Stirling Castle witnessed the first human flight in history. In 1504, one of the king's favourites was a mysterious alchemist called John Damian, Abbot of Tungland. Damian flew from the battlements using a pair of feathered wings. He fell into the castle midden or rubbish heap.

The Stewart kings also built a palace in the countryside at Falkland in Fife. This was used for banquets when the king and his courtiers went hunting in the forests there.

By 1500, Edinburgh was the capital of Scotland. When the Scottish royal family was there, they needed a suitable residence. The Royal apartments in the Castle were too cramped. The Stewarts built a new palace for themselves at Holyrood outside the city walls. Much of the building was done from 1501 to 1505 while James IV was king. He wanted to build a palace for his queen, Margaret. Later kings and queens of Scotland added to the palace. It was built in the fashionable French style. Holyrood Palace still looks like a castle because it has towers and battlements.

Holyrood Palace has towers and battlements but was never used as a castle. It is still used by the royal family when they visit Edinburgh.

Tower Houses

During the Wars of Independence, Robert the Bruce deliberately damaged the castles of Scotland. He did this so that they would be of no use to the English. After the war, he would not let the Scottish nobles rebuild their fortresses. Instead, lords and knights were encouraged to build smaller forts on their estates. These were the tower houses. They were strong enough to protect a laird and his family from outlaws but of no use to an invading army.

Many of the first tower houses were in the Borders. They were simple square towers, such as Smailholm near Roxburgh. The lower floors were used for storage and the kitchens. The laird dined with his family on the first floor. The family's sleeping quarters were at the top. There was an outer or 'barmkin' wall. This gave the tower house a small sheltered courtyard. Cattle and sheep were driven into the barmkin for safety in times of trouble.

By 1570, tower houses were being built in a new shape. This was the Z plan tower house, such as Claypotts Castle near Dundee. This style of house gave people more space and had more comfortable rooms. However, there were still shot holes in the walls. This gave the defenders a good view if there were any troublemakers outside.

Each level of a tower house was used for a different purpose.

Craigievar Castle, in
Aberdeenshire, is
slim and elegant;
the perfect Scottish
tower house.

By the 1600s, Scotland had become a much more prosperous and peaceful country. Some merchants decided to build fine houses for themselves in the country. One of these was William Forbes, known as Danzig Willie. He made a fortune trading in the Baltic Sea. In 1610, he began to build one of the most beautiful castles in the world.

This was Craigievar. Although the house was a family home, the upper floors were decorated with turrets and towers. Nevertheless, the decorative masks on the outer walls still concealed gun holes, just in case. Craigievar survives today, almost untouched since it was finished by Danzig Willie's workmen in 1626.

Victoria's Castles

In the nineteenth century, there was a great interest in everything to do with the Middle Ages. The castle style of building became very popular again in Scotland. Sir Walter Scott wrote a string of best-selling novels between 1815 and 1832. His novels were often to do with Scottish history or with the Middle Ages. Stories such as *Ivanhoe* and *Kenilworth* made the Middle Ages seem very romantic. Many wealthy people began to build country houses in the 'Romantic' fashion. Scott himself became rich from his writing. At Abbotsford in the Borders, he built a large castle-style house for himself.

In the 1840s, Queen Victoria travelled on holiday to Scotland and fell in love with the romantic appearance of the countryside. She decided to build a summer home for the Royal Family

The entrance hall at Abbotsford shows Sir Walter Scott's interest in medieval castles.

somewhere in Scotland. Victoria and her husband, Albert, disguised themselves as an ordinary couple and set out in a small carriage to travel around the country. They were looking for the perfect place to build a home. Eventually, Victoria chose Balmoral near Ballater on Deeside. Victoria had a new castle built there in the Scottish Romantic style.

In the early nineteenth century, many Scottish farmers were cruelly forced from their land. They had to go to work in the factory towns near Glasgow or emigrate abroad to countries such as Canada or Australia. The land where the farmers had lived was used for grazing sheep. The profits they made from sheep farming were often spent on new mansions. The

Dunrobin Castle in the Highlands.

Sutherland family were in charge of some the worst clearances of farming people in the far north of Scotland. With their profits, they built one of the most beautiful romantic castles in the world at Dunrobin near Golspie.

Many rich people from England and abroad began to holiday in Scotland after 1840. They could journey up to the Highlands quickly, thanks to the new railways. They bought large estates, and often enjoyed themselves shooting grouse and deer on the recently cleared land. They built houses in a castle style called Scots Baronial. Ardverickie House is a good example of this beautiful style of Scottish house building.

Years of Peace and Neglect

Some of Scotland's castles disappeared many centuries ago. Aberdeen Castle was burnt down by the English in 1336 and was never rebuilt. Other castles were destroyed in later wars, centuries after they were built. Dirleton Castle near Edinburgh was one of the strongest castles in Scotland. However, in 1650, some Royalist troops sheltered in Dirleton and were surrounded by one of Cromwell's armies. Dirleton was badly damaged by artillery fire.

Sometimes castles were pulled down by their owners and newer buildings were built on the site. Huntly Castle was originally a motte and bailey. By 1150, this was replaced by a stone keep. In the 1550s, the Earl of Huntly tore down the keep, and in its place he raised a magnificent Renaissance palace in the popular French style.

Dirleton's walls remain strong, but inside, the castle is now a ruin.

After 1650, Scotland was usually peaceful and prosperous. Many Scottish lairds had enough money to leave their old towers and build new mansion houses. Often the old stones were taken from the castle walls to build the foundations of the new house.

When lairds left their old castles, the buildings were often stripped of anything useful. Lead and slates were taken from the roofs and used on the new farmhouses that were being built in the countryside. It did not take long for the Scottish weather to turn the rest of the castle into a ruin. Old castles were an easy source of ready-cut stone. The castle of Kincardine was once one of the biggest in the kingdom. Nothing remains of Kincardine Castle today. Over the years, local farmers took the castle to pieces and used the stones to build stone dykes around their fields.

Today, Scotland's castles are better protected. Many ruined castles are cared for by Historic Scotland, a

The National Trust for Scotland has restored Fyvie Castle to its seventeenth-century splendour.

government agency that looks after our heritage. The National Trust for Scotland is a charity that also protects many of the most famous castles. Some ancient families still live in their ancestral homes. In recent years, many smaller ruined castles have been repaired and turned into homes again.

Glossary

Allies Friends in wartime.

Ambassadors Messengers sent on behalf of a king or a country.

Artillery Heavy guns.

Burgh A Scottish town, usually with the right to trade goods at market.

Chamberlain A trusted servant who ran the castle when the laird was away.

Citadel A safe fortress, usually in or very near to a town.

Clan A Highland tribe or group of families linked to the same chief.

Courtiers Attendants and servants at the royal palace.

Crag A steep rocky point on a hilltop.

Curtain wall A surrounding wall of stone which protects the inner bailey.

Earl An important Scottish nobleman, usually related to the king.

Emigrate To leave one country and live in another.

Flanders A rich area of Europe in the Middle Ages, now part of Belgium.

Garrison Soldiers who live in and protect a castle.

Gatehouse A strong building protecting the entrance to a castle.

Kinsmen Relatives.

Mercat Cross A stone pillar that marked the spot where merchants traded.

Norse People of western and central Scandinavia who raided and settled in Britain between AD 800 and 1150.

Outlaws Robbers and thieves who broke the king's law.

Palisade A high fence made of sharpened wooden stakes.

Pedlars Travelling traders who sell small items such as ribbons.

Renaissance The new age of learning and science which began around AD 1450.

Saltire The national flag of Scotland; the blue and white cross of St Andrew.

Spit-boys Kitchen servants in charge of roasting meat.

Stewart A Norman family who became Kings of Scotland and of Britain.

Stockade A high fence made of sharpened wooden stakes.

Sword of state A symbol of the Scottish kings.

Traitor Someone who helps an enemy against his own side.

Treason The act of betraying your king or country in wartime.

Wars of Independence The struggle of the Scots to stay free from England, 1296–1357.

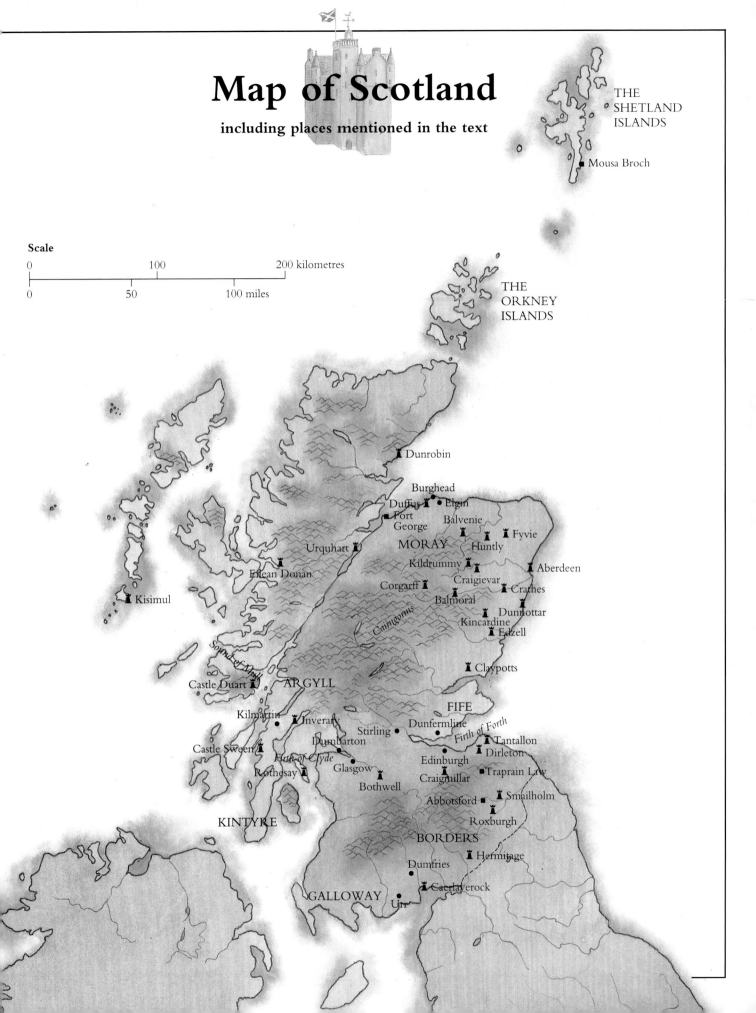

Map of Scotland
including places mentioned in the text

THE SHETLAND ISLANDS

■ Mousa Broch

THE ORKNEY ISLANDS

Scale

0   100   200 kilometres

0   50   100 miles

Dunrobin

Burghead
Duffus • Elgin
Fort George   Balvenie
MORAY   Huntly   Fyvie
Urquhart
Kildrummy   Aberdeen
Eilean Donan   Corgarff   Craigievar   Crathes
Kisimul   Balmoral   Dunnottar
Kincardine   Edzell

Cairngorms

Claypotts

Sound of Mull

Castle Duart   ARGYLL   FIFE

Kilmartin   Inverary   Stirling   Dunfermline   *Firth of Forth*
Dumbarton   Tantallon
Castle Sween   *Firth of Clyde*   Dirleton
Rothesay   Glasgow   Edinburgh   Traprain Law
Bothwell   Craigmillar
Abbotsford   Smailholm
KINTYRE   Roxburgh
BORDERS   Hermitage
Dumfries
GALLOWAY   Caerlaverock
Urr

Books to Read

For pupils:

A History of Scotland Books 2 & 3 by William Moffat (Oxford University Press, 1984)

Castle Under Siege by Richard Dargie (Wayland, 1998)

Edinburgh Castle by Chris Tabraham (Historic Scotland, 1996)

Scottish Castles by Georgeana Phillips (Richard Drew Publishing, 1987)

Scotland in the Middle Ages 400–1450 by Richard Dargie (Pulse Publications, 1995)

For teachers:

The Castles of Scotland by Maurice Lindsay (Constable Publishers, 1986)

Scottish Castles and Fortifications by Chris Tabraham (Historic Scotland, 1986)

BBC Education Scotland Resources

BBC Education Scotland has produced a range of resources on Scottish Castles.

For radio – *Castles*, a unit of stories from castles around Scotland in the series *Scottish Resources: 7–9* (Transmission Radio 3 FM, Autumn 1996. Repeat Autumn 1998)
Castle Adventure, a drama role-play unit in *Scottish Resources: 7–9* (Transmission Radio 3 FM, Spring 1999)

Radio cassettes of programmes are available for sale at time of transmission.

For TV – *Scottish Castles*, a unit in the series *See You See Me* (Transmission BBC 2, Autumn 1998)

Information on programmes and on ordering radio cassettes or print support materials is available from:
BBC Education, Room 305,
5 Queen Street, Edinburgh EH2 1JF
Tel: 0131 248 4261

Index